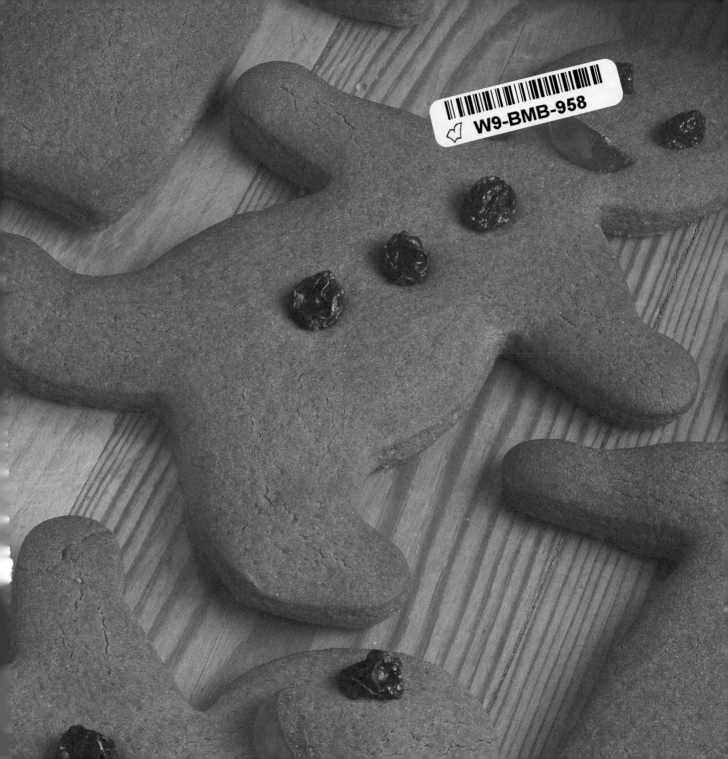

CHRISTMAS COOKIES

AND OTHER HOLIDAY BAKING TREATS

TMAS
KIES

HOLIDAY BAKING TREATS

HAMLYN

First published in 1996
by Hamlyn
an imprint of Reed Consumer Books Limited
Michelin House, 81 Fulham Road, London SW3 6RB
and Auckland, Melbourne, Singapore and Toronto

0 600 59072 0

Printed in Hong Kong

Notes
1 Use whole milk unless otherwise stated.
2 Use sweet (unsalted) butter unless otherwise stated.

Contents

Christmas Cookies

Equipment

You can make all the recipes in this book with the simplest equipment: measuring cups and spoons, bowls and mixing spoons, a saucepan, muffin tins, cake pans and baking sheets, a knife or spatula, and a wire cooling rack. However, a food processor makes the work easier, and special cookie cutters make the cookies more decorative.

For measuring
Deep-bowled metal spoons in graduated sizes are best for measuring small quantities of both liquid and dry ingredients. Straight-rimmed measuring cups make it easy to level off dry ingredients, enabling you to measure them accurately. Clearly marked heatproof glass measuring cups with a pouring spout are ideal for measuring liquid ingredients.

For sifting
Use a sifter or a strainer to sift together flour and other dry ingredients for an even consistency.

For mixing
Fill bowls no more than three-quarters full. Clear glass bowls enable you to see that all the ingredients have been well combined. Copper bowls are ideal for whisking egg whites. Heatproof bowls can be used over a saucepan of hot water to melt chocolate if you do not have a double-boiler, but be careful that the water does not touch the bottom of the bowl.

Use wire whisks for combining dry ingredients, for beating egg whites, pastry cream and whipping cream, and for stirring batters. Use wooden spoons for creaming solids and mixing doughs, and use metal spoons for folding in egg whites.

A hand-held electric mixer takes the effort out of whisking egg whites, whipping cream and mixing small amounts of batter. A countertop mixer does the same job for larger quantities and for doughs. A food processor can chop, grate, shred and mix ingredients quickly and easily, but does not aerate the ingredients to the same degree as a mixer. Some models have special bowls and beaters for whipping cream and whisking egg whites.

For rolling

Rolling pins are available in marble, glass and a number of other materials, but the wooden ones are probably the most common. Choose a long pin, with or without handles, to make rolling out easy; dust it with flour to prevent it from sticking to the dough, and wipe it clean with a cloth rather than washing it, to prevent it from warping.

For cutting

It is fun and easy to make decorative cookies with the wide range of cookie cutters available. In addition to the round scalloped cutters in a variety of sizes and the gingerbread man, shapes particularly popular at Christmas include hearts, stars, candy canes, Christmas trees and bells.

For cookies that are really special, create your own designs – a snowman, Santa Claus, and even Santa's sleigh – make reusable templates out of cardboard. See page 10 for general instructions on making and using homemade templates.

For baking

Use heavy-duty aluminum baking sheets with only a single raised edge; rims on all sides of the sheet interfere with the heat flow and prevent the cookies from crisping properly, as well as making it difficult to remove the cookies after baking, while a single edge provides a useful grip for handling the sheet. Shiny sheets are recommended, particularly for delicate and thin cookies, because dark surfaces are such good conductors of heat that they may cause the cookies to bake too quickly and become crumbly.

Cake pans are available in a range of shapes and sizes: round and square, shallow and deep. Muffin tins also come in different sizes and have a varying number of cups. A madeleine pan has shell-shaped molds for these special cookies.

Parchment paper is a non-stick, ovenproof paper ideal for lining baking sheets and cake pans. When baking cookies in batches, be sure to cool the baking sheet under cold running water and dry it thoroughly after each batch. This is not necessary if you place each batch of cookies on a piece of foil on top of the baking sheet; when one batch is done, remove it on the foil, then place the next piece of prepared foil on the baking sheet and put it in the oven immediately. Remember to keep the oven door closed to maintain the temperature while you prepare the next batch.

Foil can also be used to line cake pans for brownies and bar cookies. Use a piece of foil large enough to cover the bottom and the sides of the pan. Place it in the center of the pan, shiny side up, and press it as smooth and flat as possible over the bottom and the sides; fold the excess over the top. After the brownies or bars have cooled in the pan, lift out the foil lining and peel it away.

For cooling

A wire rack with the wires fairly close together or in a grid supports cookies, muffins and cakes while allowing the air to circulate around them. Use a spatula to transfer cookies and bars from the baking sheet to the rack.

For piping

Pastry bags can be used for piping cookies as well as for piping icing on top of them. You can buy reusable fabric or plastic pastry bags with a selection of metal tips. A coupler enables you to change the tip without emptying or changing the bag. You can buy additional tips in different sizes and shapes, but be sure you buy tips that fit your particular coupler.

If you prefer to use disposable pastry bags, cut a corner off the bottom of a large reclosable freezer bag and insert the appropriate metal tip or coupler.

You can also make your own disposable pastry bags out of baking parchment or a double thickness of waxed paper. Cut a square of paper in half diagonally, or fold it in half if using a double thickness. Put your finger in the middle of the long side to hold the paper steady. Bring one corner up to the point opposite your finger and hold these two points together. Wrap the remaining corner around the cone to meet the other two; the tip of the cone should be tightly closed. Fold the corners over the outside of the cone and staple them in position. Tape the seam closed, and put a strip of tape around the cone just above the tip to reinforce it.

Press the tip of the cone flat and cut it off. Cut straight across to make a plain round opening; make a tiny opening if you are piping chocolate, and a larger one for icing. To make a star-shaped tip, cut an inverted V into the tip. To make a rosette-shaped tip, cut an inverted W into the tip. If you are planning to use a metal tip, cut an opening large enough to hold it, but not so large that it will be pushed through when you put pressure on the contents of the bag. Before you begin decorating make enough cones for all the colors of icing and shapes of piping you want to use so that you do not have to interrupt your decorating to make more.

Techniques

Making drop cookies

Scoop up the batter with a spoon, and use your finger or a second spoon to push it off onto the baking sheet. You can leave the balls as they are, or flatten them. The easiest way to flatten them

is to lightly grease the bottom of a glass, or dust it with flour or confectioners' sugar for light-colored doughs, or cocoa for dark or chocolate doughs, and press it down gently on the dough. You can also flatten the cookies with a spatula dipped in ice water.

Shaping cookies by hand

Chill the dough so that it is firm yet pliable. If it cracks when you try to use it, let it sit at room temperature for about 15 minutes. When you are shaping light-colored doughs, dust your hands with flour or confectioners' sugar; when you are shaping dark or chocolate cookies, dust your hands with cocoa. Use a teaspoon of dough for each cookie.

TO MAKE ROUND, FLAT COOKIES, roll the dough into balls, flatten them between your palms and place them on the baking sheets.

TO MAKE ROUND COOKIES THAT CAN BE FILLED, roll the dough into balls, place them on the baking sheet, and press a well in the center of each one with your thumb.

TO MAKE A CRESCENT, roll the dough between your palms to make a short, thick rope. Pull each end of the rope to taper it, bend the whole piece into a crescent shape and place it on the baking sheet.

TO MAKE A RING, roll the dough between your palms to make a rope. Bend it into a circle and join the ends, place it on the baking sheet and flatten it gently with the palm of your hand.

Piping decorations

Practice piping before you begin decorating your cookies. You will need to be able to sustain an even pressure to create lines, and to vary the pressure to create fancier effects.

Wipe the tip clean before you begin piping. Place the point of the tip on the cookie. Exert a steady pressure on the bag, and gently lift the tip off the surface as the icing emerges. For straight lines, keep the tip about 1-inch from the surface: it is easier to keep the line straight and to move it before it touches the surface if it is crooked. To stop, break off the icing with a quick, sharp up-and-down movement. Remove any excess icing with a small skewer. Refold the top of the bag to push the icing down, and wipe the tip clean.

Using cookie cutters

Press the cutter into the dough and remove it; this should leave a trace of grease on the edges. Roll out the dough to the required thickness. Dip the edges of the cutter into flour, and tap the side of the cutter to remove any excess. Press the cutter firmly into the dough until it reaches the surface underneath. Turn the cutter slightly from side to side and lift. Tap the cutter gently with the handle of a wooden spoon to release the dough if it sticks.

Using homemade templates

A template is a pattern used to make identical copies. When planning and drawing your own designs, make the shapes clear and the edges sharp; very intricate shapes are difficult to trace around in the dough and may be lost when the dough spreads during baking. Draw the patterns on paper first, then trace them onto thick cardboard and cut them out.

To use your templates, grease or flour one side. Roll out the dough to the required thickness. Place the greased or floured side of the template onto the dough and use a very sharp, pointed knife to cut around the outline. The templates can be reused many times.

Baking

Always space cookies evenly on the baking sheet, and do not leave any large empty spaces. If you have too few cookies to fill a baking sheet, turn a pie pan or other small baking pan upside down and bake the cookies on it.

Place the baking sheet or pan in the center of the oven. If possible, turn the sheet around halfway through baking to ensure even browning.

Using a pastry bag or cone

Hold the bag about halfway down and fold the top over your wrist to form a deep cuff. Fill the pastry bag half to two-thirds full, and push the dough or icing into the tip with a small spatula. Unfold the cuff, hold the bag firmly just above the dough or icing, and press the contents down to the tip to get rid of any air bubbles. Do this every time you refill the bag to prevent an air bubble being trapped between the old and the new dough or icing, and bursting out as you are piping, ruining your work.

Place your thumb and forefinger around the top of the contents in the bag, and twist the bag twice to close it. Hold the twist tightly with your thumb and forefinger, and position your other fingers along the side of the bag. Use the fingers of your other hand to guide the tip.

Hold a homemade pastry cone near the bottom and fill it half full. Push the dough or icing into the tip with a small spatula. Close the cone and smooth the contents from the top towards the tip to get rid of any air bubbles. Fold the top over several times until it is pressing on the dough or icing. Hold the cone in the palm of your hand with your thumb on the folded end and your fingers around the side. Use the fingers of your other hand to guide the tip.

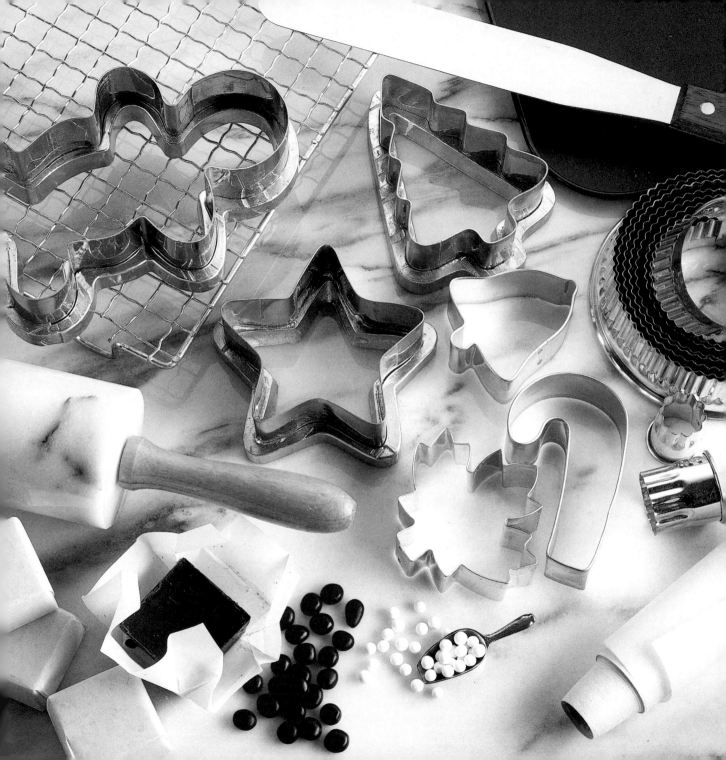

ANGEL COOKIES

½ cup, plus 1 tablespoon butter
½ cup sugar
2–3 teaspoons grated lemon zest or
¼ teaspoon vanilla extract
2 egg yolks
2 cups all-purpose flour, sifted
colored sugar crystals

1 Cream the butter with the sugar and lemon zest or vanilla extract. Gradually beat in the egg yolks, then the flour, and mix to a dough. Knead lightly. Refrigerate for 30 minutes or until stiff.
2 Roll out the dough thinly on a lightly floured surface, using a floured rolling pin. Brush off any flour on top of the dough. Using a cookie cutter or a cardboard template and a sharp knife, cut out angel shapes. Place the cookies on a sheet of foil and refrigerate until stiff.
3 Preheat the oven to 350°F, and lightly grease 2 baking sheets. Place the cookies on the baking sheets about 2 inches apart and sprinkle with colored sugar crystals. Bake for about 10 minutes, or until set and golden. Transfer to a wire rack to cool.

Makes about 24
Preparation time: 20 minutes, plus refrigerating
Cooking time: about 10 minutes

SPICED CHRISTMAS COOKIES

6 eggs
2 tablespoons dark brown sugar
2 cups all-purpose flour, sifted
scant 1 tablespoon ground cinnamon
2 teaspoons ground allspice
8 oz semisweet chocolate, grated
2 cups walnuts, broken

Icing:
2 cups confectioners' sugar
a few drops of lemon juice

1 Preheat the oven to 350°F, and grease and flour a 9 x 13-inch baking sheet.
2 Separate 2 of the eggs and reserve the whites for the icing. Beat the yolks with the whole eggs. Gradually mix in the sugar, flour, and spices until smooth. Stir in the chocolate and the walnuts.
3 Spread the mixture on the baking sheet and bake for 25–35 minutes. Cool on the sheet, then cut into squares.
4 To make the icing, sift the confectioners' sugar into a bowl, then gradually beat it into the reserved egg whites until smooth. Stir in the lemon juice. Put the icing in a pastry bag with a small tip, and pipe Christmas decorations onto the cookies.

Makes about 30
Preparation time: 15 minutes
Cooking time: 25–35 minutes

CHRISTMAS LANTERNS

⅓ cup firmly packed dark brown sugar
3 tablespoons dark molasses
a pinch of ground cinnamon
a pinch of ground cloves
a pinch of ground ginger
3 tablespoons butter
¾ teaspoon baking soda
2 teaspoons cold water
2 cups all-purpose flour, sifted
I small egg yolk
4 each of red, yellow, purple and green
clear hard candies, halved
6 red clear hard candies
ribbon, for decorating

1 Preheat the oven to 350°F, and line 2 baking sheets with parchment paper.

2 Place the sugar, molasses, spices and butter in a saucepan and heat gently until melted, stirring occasionally. Remove from the heat. Blend the baking soda with half the water and add to the saucepan with the flour and the egg yolk, and mix to a soft dough.

3 Knead on a lightly floured surface until smooth. Add more flour to the surface if necessary and roll out the dough to about ¼-inch thick. Cut out 32 2-inch squares. Cut the center from each square, leaving a ½-inch frame. Knead all the scraps together and reserve.

4 Place the frames on the baking sheets. Place half of a colored candy inside each frame. Bake in the oven for 15–20 minutes or until the candies have melted and filled the frames. Let cool completely and then remove from the paper.

5 Roll out the trimmings to a 10-inch square and cut out 16 x 2 ½-inch squares. Using the widest end of a ½-inch pastry-bag tip, cut out 8 circles from the remaining scraps. Cut out the centers of the circles with the narrow end of the tip. Place the squares and rings on a lightly floured baking sheet and bake for 15–20 minutes.

6 Place the 6 red hard candies and the remaining water in a heatproof bowl over a saucepan of boiling water until melted.

7 Use a toothpick to spread the melted candy on 2 parallel edges of 4 cookies with different colored centers, and press the cookies together to make a 4-sided frame. Continue to use the melted candy as glue, and attach a solid square cookie to the top and bottom of the frame, and a ring to the top of the assembled lantern. Make 8 lanterns in this way. Tie the ribbon through the rings on top of the lanterns. Wrap in plastic wrap or cellophane to store.

Makes 8
Preparation time: 40 minutes
Cooking time: 30–40 minutes

SNOWMAN COOKIES

½ cup all-purpose flour, sifted
2 tablespoons butter or margarine
⅛ cup sugar
I egg, beaten

Icing:
½ cup confectioners' sugar, sifted
1–2 teaspoons warm water

To Decorate:
chocolate chips
sugar sprinkles
silver and sugar balls
candied cherries

1 Preheat the oven to 350°F, and lightly grease a baking sheet.
2 Place the flour in a bowl and rub in the butter or margarine until the mixture resembles bread crumbs. Stir in the sugar and enough beaten egg to mix to a firm dough.
3 Knead the dough on a lightly floured surface until smooth. Roll out to ¼-inch thick and place on the baking sheet.
4 If you don't have a cutter, cut a snowman shape out of cardboard. Grease or flour one side. Press the greased or floured side down on the dough and cut around it with a sharp knife.
5 Bake for 12–15 minutes, until golden. Cool on the baking sheet.
6 To make the icing, place the confectioners' sugar in a bowl and gradually add the water until the mixture coats the back of a spoon thickly.
7 Cover each cookie with icing. Decorate with chocolate chips, sprinkles and silver and sugar dragées. Use slivers of candied cherries for the mouth.

Makes 10–15
Preparation time: 15 minutes
Cooking time: 12–15 minutes

MACAROONS

⅔ cup ground almonds
½ cup sugar
2 egg whites
½ teaspoon almond extract
10 whole almonds

1 Preheat the oven to 350°F. Line a baking sheet with rice paper.
2 Mix together the ground almonds and sugar. Whisk the egg whites until stiff. Fold the almond mixture and the almond extract into the egg whites.
3 Place the mixture in a pastry bag fitted with a large plain tip. Pipe 10 rounds about 2 inches across and 2 inches apart onto the baking sheet. Press an almond into the center of each one.
4 Bake for 20–25 minutes, until lightly browned and firm. Transfer to a wire rack to cool, and then trim off the extra rice paper.

Makes 10
Preparation time: 15 minutes
Cooking time: 20–25 minutes

SANTA CLAUS COOKIES

⅓ cup butter, softened
½ cup sugar
I small egg, plus I egg yolk
I ½ cups all-purpose flour, sifted

Icing:
¾ cup confectioners' sugar, sifted
about I tablespoon warm water
red food coloring

1 Preheat the oven to 350°F, and lightly grease a baking sheet.
2 Cream the butter and sugar until the mixture is light and fluffy. Mix in the eggs and then gradually beat in the flour. Using your hands, fold the dough several times.
3 Roll out the dough on a lightly floured surface to about ¼-inch thick. Cut out gingerbread-man shapes. Make hats from the scraps and press 1 onto the head of each cookie.
4 Place the cookies on the baking sheet about 2 inches apart. Bake for 10–20 minutes, till golden brown. Move to a wire rack to cool.
5 To make the icing, add enough water to the confectioners' sugar to give a smooth spreading consistency. Place one-quarter of the icing in a pastry bag fitted with a small plain tip. Add a few drops of red food coloring to the rest. Spread red icing onto the figures for Santa's suit and hat. Let it dry. Then pipe on white icing for Santa's mustache and beard, and the trim on his hat and jacket.

Makes about 15
Preparation time: 15–20 minutes
Cooking time: 10–20 minutes

PRETZELS

2 ½ cups all-purpose flour, sifted
I egg yolk
½ cup sugar
¾ cup butter, cut into flakes
13 oz frozen puff pastry, defrosted
I egg yolk, beaten
apricot jam, warmed and strained

1 Mix the flour with the egg yolk, sugar and butter to form a dough. Wrap the dough in foil and refrigerate for 2 hours.
2 Preheat the oven to 425°F, and lightly grease 2 baking sheets. Roll out the puff pastry to 20 x 14 inches. Roll out the dough to the same size, brush it with egg yolk, lay the puff pastry on top, and press together. Cut lengthwise into ¾-inch wide strips and twist into spirals, puff pastry outermost. Press the ends together, bend into pretzels, and let stand on the baking sheets for 15 minutes.
3 Bake for 15 minutes. Brush the jam onto the pretzels while warm.

Makes 18
Preparation time: 20 minutes, plus refrigerating
Cooking time: 15 minutes a batch

CHOCOLATE CHIP COOKIES

1 ¼ cups all-purpose flour
½ teaspoon baking soda
½ teaspoon salt
½ cup butter or margarine
⅔ cup sugar
1 egg
1 teaspoon vanilla extract
1 cup semisweet chocolate chips
¾ cup chopped walnuts

1 Preheat the oven to 375°F. Lightly grease 2 or more baking sheets.
2 Sift the flour, baking soda and salt together into a bowl. In another bowl, cream the butter with the sugar until the sugar has dissolved. Add the egg and beat until fluffy. Add the flour mixture, vanilla extract, chocolate chips and nuts. Drop the dough by rounded teaspoons on the baking sheets about 2 inches apart.
3 Bake for 8–10 minutes, or until browned. Transfer the cookies to a wire rack to cool.

Makes about 48
Preparation time: 15 minutes
Cooking time: 8–10 minutes a batch

CHRISTMAS TREE COOKIE DECORATIONS

¼ cup molasses
½ cup butter or margarine
4 cardamom seeds, kernels finely crushed
¼ cup sugar
2 tablespoons ground almonds
2 cups all-purpose flour
½ teaspoon baking soda
½ teaspoon ground cinnamon
½ teaspoon ground ginger
1 egg yolk
colored string, for tying

Icing:
¾ cup confectioners' sugar, sifted
about 1 tablespoon warm water

1 Melt the molasses and butter in a saucepan, stirring to combine. Stir in the crushed cardamom kernels, sugar and ground almonds. Sift in the flour, baking soda and spices, add the egg yolk and mix to a smooth dough. Wrap in foil and refrigerate for 20 minutes.
2 Preheat the oven to 375°F, and lightly grease 2 or more baking sheets. Roll out the dough on a lightly floured surface to about ¼-inch thick. Using cookie cutters, cut out Christmas trees, stars, bells and candy canes. Place on the baking sheets about 2 inches apart and bake for 10–12 minutes or until just firm.
3 Immediately make a hole at the top of each cookie with a skewer. When the cookies are firmer, move to a wire rack to cool.
4 To make the icing, add enough water to the confectioners' sugar to give a smooth spreading consistency. Place in a pastry bag fitted with a plain tip and pipe decorations onto each cookie.
5 Carefully thread a piece of colored string through the hole in the cookies, tie firmly and hang the cookies on the Christmas tree.

Makes about 30
Preparation time: 20 minutes, plus refrigerating
Cooking time: 10–12 minutes a batch

17

PINWHEEL COOKIES

¾ cup dates, stoned and chopped
⅓ cup sugar
½ cup water
¼ cup blanched almonds, finely chopped
1 cup self-rising flour
¼ teaspoon salt
¼ teaspoon baking powder
¼ cup butter
⅓ cup sugar
1 egg yolk

1 Put the dates in a saucepan with the sugar and water. Simmer over a low heat until the mixture thickens. Remove from the heat, cool, and then stir in the almonds.
2 Sift the flour, salt and baking powder together into a bowl. In another bowl, cream the butter and the sugar. Beat in the egg yolk, then stir in the flour mixture. Knead to a smooth dough, wrap in foil and refrigerate for 1 hour.
3 Roll out the dough on a lightly floured surface to about 8 x 14 inches. Spread the date mixture evenly on top. Roll up the dough, starting at a short side. Wrap in foil and refrigerate for 3–4 hours.
4 Preheat the oven to 375°F, and grease 2 baking sheets. Cut the roll into ¼-inch slices. Place on the baking sheets 2 inches apart and bake for 10–12 minutes, or until golden. Cool on the baking sheets for 1 minute, then move to a wire rack to cool completely.

Makes about 30
Preparation time: 30 minutes, plus refrigerating
Cooking time: 10–12 minutes a batch

CHRISTMAS TREE SHAPED COOKIES

1 ½ cups all-purpose flour, sifted
½ cup butter or margarine
¼ cup sugar
½ teaspoon ground cinnamon
2–3 tablespoons grated orange zest
1 egg yolk

To Decorate:
2 cups confectioners' sugar, sifted
2–3 tablespoons orange juice
coarsely grated orange zest

1 Preheat the oven to 350°F, and lightly grease 2 baking sheets.
2 Place the flour into a bowl and rub in the butter until the mixture resembles bread crumbs. Add the sugar, cinnamon, orange zest and egg yolk, and mix to a smooth dough.
3 Knead lightly, then roll out on a lightly floured surface to about ¼-inch thick. Using a cookie cutter, cut out Christmas tree shapes. Place on the baking sheets about 2 inches apart and bake for 10–15 minutes, until golden. Transfer to a wire rack to cool.
4 Mix the confectioners' sugar with the orange juice until smooth and use to coat the top of the cookies. Sprinkle with orange zest.

Makes 24
Preparation time: 15 minutes
Cooking time: 10–15 minutes

ANISEED COOKIES

2 ½ cups all-purpose flour
¾ teaspoon baking powder
½ teaspoon salt
½ cup butter, at room temperature
½ cup lard
1 cup sugar
2 teaspoons whole aniseed
2 eggs, beaten
confectioners' sugar, sifted

1 Preheat the oven to 375°F. Lightly grease 2 baking sheets.
2 Sift the flour, baking powder and salt together into a bowl. In another bowl, cream the butter and lard with the sugar until light and fluffy. Beat in the aniseed and the eggs. Add the flour mixture and mix to a soft dough. If it is too sticky, add a little more flour.
3 Divide the dough in half and, on a surface lightly covered with confectioners' sugar, roll out each piece to about ¼-inch thick. Cut out Christmas shapes with cookie cutters or a knife, and place on the baking sheets about 2 inches apart. Alternatively, roll teaspoons of dough into balls, place on the baking sheets 2 inches apart and flatten with a fork.
4 Bake for about 10 minutes, or until the edges of the cookies are just tinged brown. Cool on the baking sheets for 2–3 minutes, then transfer to wire racks to cool completely.

Makes about 60, depending on shape
Preparation time: 15 minutes
Cooking time: 10 minutes a batch

PEANUT BUTTER COOKIES

2 ½ cups all-purpose flour
½ teaspoon baking powder
½ teaspoon salt
½ teaspoon baking soda
½ cup margarine, diced
1 ⅓ cups firmly packed light brown sugar
generous ⅓ cup crunchy peanut butter
2 eggs, beaten

1 Preheat the oven to 400°F. Lightly grease 2 baking sheets.
2 Sift the flour, baking powder, salt and baking soda together into a bowl. Rub in the margarine until the mixture resembles bread crumbs. Stir in the sugar. Add the peanut butter and eggs, and mix to a soft dough.
3 Roll the dough into balls about 1-inch across, and place them on the baking sheets about 2 inches apart. Press the surface of each cookie with a fork to make a crisscross pattern.
4 Bake for 12–15 minutes until risen. Cool on the baking sheets for 1 minute, then transfer to a wire rack to cool completely.

Makes about 50
Preparation time: 25 minutes
Cooking time: 12–15 minutes a batch

BRANDY SNAPS

½ cup butter
½ cup turbinado sugar or ⅔ cup firmly packed dark brown sugar
⅓ cup corn syrup
I cup all-purpose flour
I teaspoon ground ginger
2 teaspoons brandy

I Preheat the oven to 350°F. Grease 2 or more baking sheets and the handle of a wooden spoon.

2 Put the butter, sugar and corn syrup into a saucepan and heat gently until the butter has melted and the sugar has dissolved. Let cool slightly, then sift in the flour and ginger, add the brandy, and beat the mixture well.

3 Drop the mixture by rounded teaspoons on the baking sheets at least 4 inches apart, and bake for 10–12 minutes, until golden.

4 Let cool slightly, then remove with a spatula and roll around the handle of the wooden spoon. Let set for 1–2 minutes, then carefully slip the cookie onto a wire rack to cool.

Makes 35
Preparation time: 15 minutes, plus cooling
Cooking time: 10–12 minutes a batch

BUTTER COOKIES

¼ cup butter
½ cup confectioners' sugar
2 tablespoons superfine sugar
I egg, beaten
½ cup all-purpose flour, sifted

I Preheat the oven to 425°F. Line 2 baking sheets with parchment paper.

2 Beat the butter until soft. Sift the sugars together, then beat into the butter for about 2 minutes, until creamy. Slowly add the egg to the mixture, beating constantly. Fold in the flour.

3 Spoon the mixture into a pastry bag fitted with a small round tip and pipe small rounds onto the paper, spacing them about 1-inch apart. Bake for 4–6 minutes, until the edges turn golden brown. Let cool slightly, then transfer to a wire rack to cool completely.

Makes about 30
Preparation time: 10 minutes
Cooking time: 4–6 minutes a batch

GINGERBREAD PEOPLE

2 cups all-purpose flour
I teaspoon ground ginger
½ cup butter or margarine
⅔ cup firmly packed dark brown sugar
⅓ cup molasses

To Decorate:
raisins
candied fruit peel

I Preheat the oven to 375°F, and lightly grease a baking sheet.
2 Sift the flour and ginger into a bowl together. In another bowl cream the butter with the sugar until light and fluffy. Add the flour mixture and the molasses, mix, and then knead until smooth.
3 Roll out the dough on a lightly floured surface to about ¼-inch thick. Cut out gingerbread people. Press in raisins for eyes and a row of buttons. Use candied fruit peel for the mouth.
4 Place on the baking sheet and bake for 20 minutes.

Makes 6
Preparation time: 10–15 minutes
Cooking time: 20 minutes

GINGERBREAD TREE DECORATIONS

2 cups all-purpose flour
2 teaspoons ground ginger
½ cup butter, diced
I cup firmly packed light brown sugar
I egg, beaten
sugar sprinkles, to decorate
ribbon, for tying

Icing:
I egg white
2 cups confectioners' sugar, sifted
½ teaspoon lemon juice
I drop glycerin

I Sift the flour and ginger into a bowl. Add the butter and rub it in until the mixture resembles fine bread crumbs. Stir in the sugar and enough of the egg to make a stiff dough. Knead the dough quickly on a lightly floured surface until smooth. Shape into a roll about 1-inch in diameter, wrap in foil and refrigerate until chilled.
2 Preheat the oven to 350°F. Lightly grease 2 or more baking sheets. Roll out the dough to ¼-inch thick. Cut out Christmas shapes. Make a hole at the top of each cookie. Place the cookies on the baking sheets and refrigerate for 10 minutes. Bake for 15–20 minutes, or until golden. Cool slightly, then move to a rack.
3 To make the icing, whisk the egg white until frothy. Gradually beat in about half the confectioners' sugar, then add the lemon juice and glycerin, and gradually beat in the remaining sugar. Cover the bowl with a damp cloth and set aside for 10 minutes.
4 Dip the cookies in the icing, sprinkle with sugar sprinkles, and leave to dry. Thread the ribbon through the holes and tie.

Makes about 30
Preparation time: 20 minutes, plus refrigerating
Cooking time: 15–20 minutes a batch

CHRISTMAS GINGERBREAD HOUSE

I ½ lb (6 cups) all-purpose flour
3 teaspoons baking soda
3 teaspoons ground ginger
I cup margarine, diced
I ⅔ cups firmly packed dark brown sugar
½ cup corn syrup
2 eggs, lightly beaten

Icing:
I egg white
2 cups confectioners' sugar, sifted
I teaspoon lemon juice

To Decorate:
hard candies
chocolate flakes or sugar sprinkles
chocolate-covered orange peel
or small chocolate cookies
miniature candy canes

1 Preheat the oven to 375°F, and lightly grease 2 baking sheets.
2 To make the patterns, draw the shapes on graph paper (the scale of the figure is 1 square = 1-inch). Use carbon paper to trace them onto stiff cardboard. Label all the pieces so that you can easily identify each one. Grease or flour the other side of each pattern.
3 To make the gingerbread, sift the flour, baking soda and ground ginger into a bowl together. Rub in the margarine until the mixture resembles bread crumbs. Add the sugar and mix well.
4 Warm the syrup to make it flow easily and stir it into the mixture with the eggs to make a soft, pliable dough. Knead the dough until smooth.
5 Roll out the dough to about ¼-inch thick on the baking sheets. Press the greased or floured side of the patterns down on the dough and cut around them with a sharp knife. Remove the scraps. Cut a heart-shaped window out of the front gable and place 1 hard candy in the middle; it will melt during baking to make a colored window.
6 Bake for about 10 minutes, until the gingerbread is evenly colored. If any piece has become misshapen during baking, place the relevant pattern on top of it and trim the edges while the cookie is still warm. Let the pieces cool for up to 24 hours before starting to assemble the house.
7 To make the icing, whisk the egg white to a light froth and beat in the confectioners' sugar 1 spoonful at a time. Beat in the lemon juice. Do not try to beat the mixture too stiffly; it should be soft enough to hang from the eaves like melting snow.
8 Assemble the house on a 12-inch diameter cake board. Fill a pastry bag fitted with a plain tip with icing. Apply the icing to the bottom edge and inner wall of 1 side of the house. Quickly apply icing to the bottom edge of 1 gable end, and position it on the board with the side. The icing will hold them in place. Quickly apply icing to the second gable end and fix in position in the same way. Then apply icing to the bottom edge and inner wall of the second side and attach it to the 2 gable ends. You will be able to hide any gaps at these corners with the decoration.
9 Coat the top of the walls with icing and attach the roof panels.

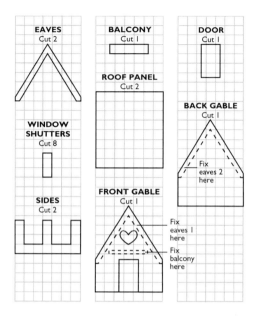

EAVES
Cut 2

BALCONY
Cut 1

DOOR
Cut 1

ROOF PANEL
Cut 2

BACK GABLE
Cut 1

WINDOW SHUTTERS
Cut 8

Fix eaves 2 here

SIDES
Cut 2

FRONT GABLE
Cut 1

Fix eaves 1 here

Fix balcony here

Use icing to add the balcony, window shutters, and the door in an open position, and to fix the eaves to the gables, holding each of these pieces in position until the icing begins to harden.

10 To decorate, spread icing on the roof panels and cover with chocolate flakes or sugar sprinkles, and place chocolate-covered orange peel or chocolate cookies along the ridge between the panels. Use icing to attach candy canes as balcony supports. Spread icing on the eaves and swirl it back and forth so that the eaves appear to be dripping with snow.

11 Pipe icing around the edge of the balcony, the shutters and the door. Place some hard candies inside the house so that they can be seen through the windows and door.

Makes 1
Preparation time: 1 ½ hours, plus cooling
Cooking time: 10 minutes

OATMEAL RAISIN COOKIES

¾ **cup raisins**
½ **cup hot water**
1 **cup all-purpose flour**
1 **teaspoon salt**
½ **teaspoon baking soda**
½ **teaspoon ground cinnamon**
¾ **cup butter or margarine**
1 **cup firmly packed light brown sugar**
1 **egg**
1 **teaspoon vanilla extract**
3 **cups rolled oats**

1 Preheat the oven to 350°F. Lightly grease 2 baking sheets.
2 Soak the raisins in the hot water for 15 minutes. Drain well, reserving ¼ cup of the water.
3 Sift the flour, salt, baking soda and cinnamon into a bowl together and set aside. In another bowl cream the butter or margarine with the sugar until the sugar has dissolved. Beat in the egg, vanilla extract and the reserved water until thoroughly blended. Add the flour mixture and the oats, stirring with a wooden spoon until well incorporated. Mix in the raisins.
4 Drop the dough by rounded teaspoons on the baking sheets about 1 ½ inches apart. Bake for 12–15 minutes, until golden. Transfer to a wire rack to cool.

Makes about 60
Preparation time: 15 minutes
Cooking time: 12–15 minutes a batch

MINCE PIES

2 cups self-rising flour
a pinch of salt
⅛ cup sugar
¼ cup butter, diced
¼ cup margarine, diced
⅛ cup lard, diced
1 egg yolk
milk, to mix
1 ½ cups mincemeat, to fill
1 egg white, beaten, to glaze
superfine sugar, to dredge

1 To make the pastry, sift the self-rising flour, salt and sugar together into a bowl. Rub in the butter, margarine and lard together until the mixture resembles fine bread crumbs. Add the egg yolk and enough milk to mix to a pliable dough, using a round-bladed knife.

2 Preheat the oven to 400°F, and lightly grease 2 or more muffin tins (16–18 cups).

3 Knead the dough on a lightly floured surface until smooth and even. Roll out the pastry and cut out 16–18 rounds with a fluted 3-inch cookie cutter. Cut out 16–18 slightly smaller rounds for the lids. Place the large rounds in the muffin tins and fill each one with about 2 teaspoons of mincemeat. Dampen the edges of the lids with a little cold water, place on top of the pies and press down lightly to seal.

4 Brush the tops of the mince pies with the egg white and dredge lightly with sugar. Make a small slit in the top of each mince pie and bake for about 20 minutes.

5 Let the mince pies cool slightly in the tins, then carefully transfer to a wire rack to cool completely.

Makes 16–18
Preparation time: 40 minutes
Cooking time: 20 minutes

STICKY GINGERBREAD

½ cup margarine
⅔ cup firmly packed light brown sugar
⅔ cup corn syrup
⅓ cup molasses
2 ½ cups all-purpose flour
2 teaspoons ground ginger
1 teaspoon baking soda
2 eggs, beaten
⅔ cup hot water

1 Preheat the oven to 350°F. Grease and line a 9 x 12-inch cake pan with baking parchment.

2 Place the margarine, sugar, corn syrup and molasses in a saucepan, and heat gently until the margarine has melted and the sugar has dissolved.

3 Sift the flour, ginger and baking soda together into a bowl, and make a well in the center. Pour the contents of the saucepan into the bowl and beat to mix thoroughly. Add the beaten eggs and hot water, and mix to a smooth batter

4 Pour the batter into the cake pan and bake for 45 minutes, until the cake springs back when pressed lightly. Turn out of the pan, remove the lining paper, and transfer to a wire rack to cool. Keep for 2 days before cutting into bars.

Makes about 15 bars
Preparation time: 15 minutes
Cooking time: 45 minutes

MOLASSES BARS

1 ½ cups all-purpose flour
¼ teaspoon ground cinnamon
¼ teaspoon grated nutmeg
¼ teaspoon ground allspice
¼ teaspoon ground cloves
½ teaspoon baking soda
½ cup butter
⅓ cup firmly packed light brown sugar
1 egg
¼ cup sour cream
¼ cup honey
¼ cup light molasses
1 teaspoon vanilla extract
1 teaspoon grated lemon zest
¾ cup slivered almonds

1 Preheat the oven to 350°F, and grease a 7 ½ x 11-inch shallow baking pan.

2 Sift the flour, spices and baking soda together and set aside. Beat the butter with the sugar until well creamed and the sugar has dissolved. Add the egg and sour cream, and beat well. Add the honey, molasses, vanilla extract and grated lemon zest, and continue beating until well blended. Stir in the flour mixture and half the almonds.

3 Spread the batter in the baking pan and sprinkle the remaining almonds on top. Bake for 18–20 minutes, or until a toothpick inserted into the center comes out clean. Transfer to a wire rack to cool, then cut into bars.

Makes about 20
Preparation time: 15 minutes
Cooking time: 18–20 minutes

FLORENTINES

¼ **cup butter**
¼ **cup vanilla-flavored sugar**
I tablespoon heavy cream, whipped
3 tablespoons chopped mixed peel
3 tablespoons candied cherries, washed,
dried and chopped
I ½ tablespoons candied angelica,
finely chopped
⅛ cup slivered almonds
⅛ cup all-purpose flour
6 oz semisweet chocolate, chopped

I Preheat the oven to 350°F, and grease 2 baking sheets.
2 Melt the butter slowly in a saucepan. Stir in the sugar and the cream, and slowly bring to a boil. Boil for about 1 minute, then remove from the heat. Let cool a little.
3 Stir in the fruit and nuts, and then the flour. Drop teaspoons of the dough onto the baking sheets about 3 inches apart, and bake for 10–12 minutes, until the florentines are brown at the edges. Remove from the oven and cool on the baking sheets for a few seconds, then transfer to a wire rack to cool completely. If the florentines harden while you are trying to remove them from the baking sheet, return the sheet to the oven for a few minutes and they will soften again.
4 Place the chocolate in a heatproof bowl over a saucepan of simmering water, and stir until it is melted. Spread the melted chocolate over the back of the florentines, and mark wavy lines in it with a fork while it is still soft.

Makes about 12
Preparation time: 15 minutes
Cooking time: 10–12 minutes

FLAPJACKS

½ **cup butter or margarine**
⅔ **cup firmly packed light brown sugar**
3 tablespoons corn syrup
2 ⅔ cups rolled oats

I Preheat the oven to 350°F, and grease a shallow 8-inch square cake pan.
2 Melt the butter or margarine with the sugar and corn syrup, then stir in the rolled oats and mix thoroughly. Turn into the cake pan, and smooth the top with a spatula. Bake for 25–30 minutes, until golden brown. Cut into 2-inch squares while still warm, then let cool completely before removing from the pan.

Makes 16
Preparation time: 10 minutes
Cooking time: 25–30 minutes

BLONDIES

4 oz white chocolate, roughly chopped
½ cup butter, softened
I cup sugar
2 eggs, beaten
I cup all-purpose flour, sifted
I teaspoon vanilla extract
I ⅓ cups pecan nuts, roughly chopped

I Preheat the oven to 350°F, and lightly grease a 7 x 11-inch cake pan.

2 Melt half the chocolate in a heatproof bowl over a saucepan of simmering water, stirring.

3 Cream the butter with the sugar. Add the eggs a little at a time, and then stir in the melted chocolate, the flour, the vanilla extract, the pecans and the remaining chopped chocolate. Pour the batter into the cake pan, and spread it evenly.

4 Bake for about 25 minutes, until a toothpick inserted into the center comes out clean. Let cool in the pan, then cut into 12 pieces.

Makes 12
Preparation time: 15 minutes
Cooking time: about 25 minutes

MILLIONAIRE'S SHORTBREAD

½ cup plus 2 tablespoons butter
½ cup sugar
2 ½ cups all-purpose flour

Filling:
2 tablespoons butter
½ cup sugar
2 tablespoons corn syrup
I ⅓ cups (I can) condensed milk
4 oz semisweet chocolate, chopped

I Preheat the oven to 350°F. Grease a 9 x 12-inch baking sheet.

2 Cream the butter with the sugar, then gradually work in the flour. Press the mixture evenly onto the baking sheet. Bake for 15–20 minutes, until golden. Let cool.

3 To make the filling, place the butter, sugar, syrup and condensed milk in a saucepan and heat gently until the sugar has dissolved, stirring occasionally. Increase the heat and boil for 5 minutes, stirring constantly. Remove from the heat, let stand for 1 minute, then pour onto the shortbread. Let the filling set.

4 Melt the chocolate in a heatproof bowl over a saucepan of simmering water, stirring. Spread over the filling, and mark into bars while the chocolate is still soft. Let cool completely on the baking sheet before cutting into bars.

Makes about 16
Preparation time: 40 minutes
Cooking time: about 30 minutes

FONDANT FANCIES

¼ **cup butter, softened**
¼ **cup clear honey**
1 ½ **cups all-purpose flour, sifted**
2 **teaspoons baking powder, sifted**
1 **teaspoon baking soda**
3 **tablespoons ground ginger**
scant 1 cup milk
2 **eggs, beaten**

Icing:
1 ½ **lb (6 cups) confectioners' sugar, sifted**
yellow food coloring

To Decorate:
candied angelica
candied cherries
colored sugar balls
thin satin ribbon

1 Preheat the oven to 325°F. Grease and line a 6-inch square, deep cake pan.

2 Beat the butter and honey until light and fluffy. Beat in the flour, baking powder, baking soda, ginger, milk and eggs. Spoon the batter into the cake pan and bake for 45 minutes, until well risen. Cool in the pan, then turn out and cut into 6 squares.

3 Place the confectioners' sugar in a bowl and add enough water to make a very thick, smooth icing. Transfer half the icing to another bowl and mix in the yellow food coloring. Cover the white icing with plastic wrap to prevent a crust forming.

4 Stick a large skewer or small fork into the base of a cake to hold it secure, then spoon some of the icing onto it. Smooth the icing with a warm round-bladed knife or spatula. Place the cake on a wire rack to set. Ice 3 of the cakes with yellow icing, and 3 with white, reserving a little of the icing.

5 Press candied angelica, candied cherries and colored sugar balls into the icing in an attractive pattern. Use the reserved icing to fix the ribbon around the sides of the cakes.

Makes 6
Preparation time: 40 minutes
Cooking time: 45 minutes

MILLE-FEUILLES

13 oz frozen puff pastry, defrosted
4 tablespoons strawberry jam
1 tablespoon orange juice
1 ¼ cups heavy cream
2 teaspoons superfine sugar
1 lb strawberries, halved

Icing:
⅓ cup confectioners' sugar, sifted
a little water

1 Preheat the oven to 425°F.

2 Roll out the pastry on a lightly floured surface to 8 x 10 inches. Using a very sharp knife and a single swift movement for each cut, cut the pastry lengthwise into 3 equal pieces and cut each strip into 3 widthwise to make 9 equal rectangles. Place the pastry on dampened baking sheets. Bake for 20 minutes, until risen and golden. Transfer to a wire rack to cool.

3 Trim the rectangles to the same size. Mix the jam with the orange juice. Whip the cream with the superfine sugar.

4 To assemble each mille-feuille, spread 1 side of a pastry rectangle with one-sixth of the jam. Spread one-sixth of the whipped cream on top of the jam and one-sixth of the strawberries on top of the cream. Cover with another piece of pastry and repeat the filling. Place a third piece of pastry on top.

5 Mix the confectioners' sugar with enough water to make a smooth, thick icing, and spread some on the top of the pastry.

Makes 3
Preparation time: 25 minutes
Cooking time: 20 minutes

RUGELACH

Pastry:
generous ¾ cup lightly salted
butter, softened
1 cup packaged cream cheese
2 teaspoons superfine sugar
2 cups all-purpose flour
water, to glaze
butter, softened
1 egg white beaten with
1 tablespoon water, to glaze
a little granulated sugar

Filling:
½ cup firmly packed soft light brown sugar
1 teaspoon cinnamon
¾ cup walnut halves, chopped very finely

1 Using a wooden spoon, cream the butter and cheese together in a large mixing bowl until soft and well blended. Stir in the sugar and then sift the flour over the bowl and mix in to form a dough. Form the dough into 2 balls. Wrap each in plastic wrap and refrigerate for at least 30 minutes.

2 Meanwhile mix all the ingredients for the filling together, and preheat the oven to 375°F.

3 Roll out one ball of dough as thinly as possible into a circle roughly 11 inches in diameter. Cut into a neat circle using a cake pan as a guide. Using a sharp knife, cut the dough into 16 equal wedges, as you would a pie. Brush the surface with the glaze and sprinkle it with half the filling. Cover with a piece of plastic wrap. With a rolling pin, press down on the plastic wrap to embed the filling in the dough. Remove the plastic wrap and roll the wedges, starting from the long edge, and then bend to form crescents. Place on a baking sheet. Brush the tops of all the crescents with the glaze and sprinkle them with granulated sugar. Repeat with the other ball of pastry.

4 Bake for 10–20 minutes, or until golden brown. Cool on a rack.

Makes 32
Preparation time: 30–40 minutes, plus refrigerating
Cooking time: 10–20 minutes

MINI BRIOCHES

I tablespoon active dry yeast
I ½ tablespoons warm water
I tablespoon sugar
2 cups all-purpose flour
½ teaspoon salt
2 eggs, beaten
¼ cup butter, melted
beaten egg, to glaze

I Grease 1–2 muffin tins (12 cups) with 3-inch cups.
2 Blend the yeast with the water, add 1 teaspoon of the sugar, and stand for 10 minutes. In another bowl, sift the flour, salt and remaining sugar. Add the yeast, eggs and butter, mix until smooth. Knead for 5 minutes, until smooth. Place in an oiled bowl, cover and set in a warm place until doubled in size, about 1 hour.
3 Knead the dough again for a few minutes, then divide it into 12 pieces. Shape three-quarters of each piece into a round and place it in the muffin tin. Press a hole in the center. Shape each remaining piece into a ball and place it on top of the hole. Cover and set in a warm place to rise until the dough reaches the top of the tins.
4 Preheat the oven to 450°F. Brush the top of each brioche with beaten egg and bake for 10 minutes. Transfer to a rack to cool.

Makes 12
Preparation time: 20 minutes, plus rising
Cooking time: 10 minutes

PROFITEROLES

⅔ cup water
¼ cup butter
½ cup all-purpose flour, sifted
a pinch of salt
2 eggs, lightly beaten
I cup heavy cream, lightly whipped

Caramel Sauce:
⅓ cup sugar
¼ cup cold water
⅔ cup heavy cream

I Preheat the oven to 400°F, and grease 2 baking sheets.
2 Put the water and butter in a pan, bring to a boil. Remove from the heat, add the flour and salt, and beat until the dough forms a ball. Cool slightly, then beat in the eggs to form a shiny dough.
3 Spoon the dough into a pastry bag with a 1-inch tip. Pipe small mounds onto the baking sheets. Bake for 20 minutes, until risen.
4 Transfer to a rack and split each one. Cool, then fill with cream.
5 To make the sauce, heat the sugar in a pan over a low heat until dissolved. Increase the heat and cook to a golden caramel. Remove from the heat and carefully add the water. Return to the heat and stir until the caramel dissolves. Cool, then whip in the cream. Arrange the profiteroles on a dish and spoon over the sauce.

Serves 6
Preparation time: 20 minutes, plus cooling
Cooking time: 15–20 minutes

37

PANETONNE

1 teaspoon granulated sugar
1 tablespoon active dry yeast
¼ cup warm milk
½ cup butter
¼ cup superfine sugar
3 eggs, beaten
½–¾ teaspoon grated lemon zest
3 ½ cups all-purpose flour
1 teaspoon salt
⅔ cup raisins
½ cup cut mixed peel
beaten egg, to glaze

1 Sprinkle the granulated sugar and yeast over the warm milk and leave until frothy, about 10 minutes. Cream the butter and superfine sugar together until light and fluffy. Beat in the eggs, a little at a time, then beat in the lemon zest.

2 Place the flour and salt in a large bowl. Stir in the yeast liquid and the creamed mixture, and mix to a soft dough. Knead the dough on a lightly floured surface until smooth, silky and no longer sticky. Place in a greased plastic bag and set to rise until doubled in size, about 1 hour.

3 Lightly grease an 8-inch cake pan. Sprinkle the raisins and mixed peel over the dough and knead until thoroughly mixed in. Place the dough in the cake pan and leave until doubled in size, about 45 minutes.

4 Preheat the oven to 400°F. Brush the dough with the beaten egg and bake for 10 minutes, then lower the temperature to 350°F and bake for 30 minutes, until deep golden brown and firm to the touch. A skewer should come out clean when inserted into the centre of the panetonne. Transfer to a wire rack to cool. Serve cut into slices.

Makes 1 x 8-inch cake
Preparation time: 30 minutes, plus rising
Cooking time: 40 minutes

DANISH PASTRIES

2 teaspoons active dry yeast
scant ⅓ cup hand-hot water
1 teaspoon superfine sugar
2 cups all-purpose flour, sifted
pinch of salt
2 tablespoons lard, diced
1 tablespoon granulated sugar
1 egg, beaten
½ cup plus 1 tablespoon butter

Vanilla Cream Filling:
1 tablespoon beaten egg
1 teaspoon all-purpose flour
1 teaspoon caster sugar
¼ cup milk
1 teaspoon vanilla extract

Almond Paste Filling:
¼ cup ground almonds
⅛ cup superfine sugar
1 drop almond extract
1 teaspoon beaten egg

Apple and Raisin Filling:
2 teaspoons chopped seedless raisins
2 tablespoons grated apple
¼ teaspoon grated orange zest
2 teaspoons light brown sugar
a pinch of mixed spice

Cinnamon Filling:
2 tablespoons butter
⅛ cup sugar
1 teaspoon ground cinnamon
1 teaspoon currants
1 teaspoon cut mixed peel

1 Blend the yeast with the water, add the superfine sugar, and let stand in a warm place until frothy, about 10 minutes.
2 Place the flour and salt in another bowl, and rub in the lard until the mixture resembles bread crumbs. Add the sugar, egg and yeast liquid, and mix to a soft dough. Knead gently on a lightly floured surface until smooth. Wrap in greased plastic wrap and refrigerate for 10 minutes.
3 Using a round-bladed knife, soften the butter on a plate. Roll out the dough on a lightly floured surface to a 10-inch square. In the center of the dough, about 2 ½ inches from each end, spread the butter in a 5 x 9-inch rectangle. Fold the 2 unbuttered parts of the dough over to just overlap in the center. Use a rolling pin to seal the edges.
4 Turn the dough 90° and roll it out to 5 x 15 inches. Fold the top third over the middle, then fold the bottom third over it. Place the dough on a plate, cover with greased plastic wrap and refrigerate for 10 minutes or until the butter is very firm. Repeat rolling, folding and refrigerating the dough twice more.
5 To make the Vanilla Cream Filling, mix the egg, flour and sugar together in a saucepan. Beat in the milk and bring to a boil, stirring. Remove from the heat and stir in the vanilla extract.
6 To make each of the other fillings, combine the ingredients.
7 To make the Egg Glaze, mix the ingredients together. To make the Apricot Glaze, warm the jam in a saucepan with enough water to coat the back of a spoon thinly, then strain.
8 To make the icing, mix the confectioner's sugar with enough water to coat the back of a spoon thinly.
9 Preheat the oven to 425°F, and lightly grease 2 or more baking sheets. Divide the dough into 4 equal pieces and lightly flour a surface on which to roll it out.
10 Roll out 1 piece to 4 x 8 inches, and cut into 2-inch squares. Spread one-quarter of the Apple and Raisin filling diagonally across each of 4 squares. Divide half the Vanilla Cream Filling into 4, and spread it diagonally across each of the other 4 squares. Fold over 2 opposite corners to overlap and enclose the fillings. Brush with Egg Glaze, and press lightly to seal. Place the pastries on a

Egg Glaze:
1 egg yolk, beaten
1 teaspoon superfine sugar
1 tablespoon water

Apricot Glaze:
2 tablespoons apricot jam
1–2 tablespoons water

Icing:
½ cup confectioner's sugar, sifted
1–2 tablespoons water

To Decorate:
2 apricot halves, fresh or canned, chopped
slivered almonds
candied cherries, chopped

baking sheet and set in a warm place until they are puffy, about 30 minutes.

11 Roll out 1 piece of dough to 3 x 6 inches, and cut into 1 ½-inch squares. Brush each square with Egg Glaze. Divide the chopped apricots between the squares. Fold the corners of the dough to meet in the middle and press gently to seal. Put one-eighth of the remaining Vanilla Cream Filling in the center of each square. Place the pastries on a baking sheet and set in a warm place until they are puffy, about 30 minutes.

12 Roll out 1 piece of dough to 4 x 8 inches, and cut into 2-inch squares. Brush each square with Egg Glaze. Make a ⅜-inch diagonal cut from the corners in each square towards the middle. Roll out the Almond Paste into 8 balls and place one in the centre of each square. Fold alternate points onto the filling, and press firmly to secure. Brush the folded over parts with Egg Glaze. Place the pastries on a baking sheet and set in a warm place until they are puffy, about 30 minutes.

13 Roll out the last piece of dough to 4 x 10 inches. Spread the Cinnamon Filling evenly on top, and roll up the pastry from a short side. Using a sharp knife, cut into 8 slices and place cut side down on a baking sheet. Brush the pastries with Egg Glaze and set in a warm place until they are puffy, about 30 minutes.

14 Bake the pastries for 7–10 minutes, until golden brown. While the pastries are still hot, brush the apricot-filled squares with Apricot Glaze, and then drizzle icing over all the pastries, and scatter slivered almonds on some and candied cherries on others.

Makes 32
Preparation time: 40 minutes, plus resting and refrigerating
Cooking time: 7–10 minutes a batch

MINI STOLLEN

4 teaspoons active dry yeast
2 tablespoons warm water
⅓ cup sugar
a pinch of salt
6 tablespoons warm milk
2 tablespoons rum
a few drops almond extract
3 ½ cups all-purpose flour
1 egg, beaten
¾ cup butter, softened
⅓ cup raisins
¼ cup candied cherries, chopped, washed and dried
⅓ cup currants
1 ½–2 tablespoons chopped candied angelica
⅓ cup chopped mixed peel
¼ cup slivered almonds
confectioners' sugar, sifted

1 Blend the yeast and water with 1 teaspoon of the sugar and set in a warm place until frothy. Dissolve ¼ cup of the sugar and the salt in the milk. Add the rum, almond extract and yeast liquid.
2 Sift the flour into a bowl, making a well in the center. Add the yeast mixture, egg, ⅓ cup of the butter, cut into pieces, and the raisins, candied fruit and nuts. Mix to a soft dough and knead for 10 minutes. Replace in the bowl, cover with a damp cloth and set in a warm place to rise until doubled in size, about 2 hours.
3 Lightly grease a baking sheet. Punch down the dough and knead until smooth, then roll out to about 8 x 12 inches. Melt the remaining butter and brush liberally over the dough. Sprinkle with the remaining sugar. Fold one long side over just beyond the center, and then fold the other long side to overlap the first. Press lightly together, cut into 4, and slightly taper the ends of each piece. Place on the baking sheet, brush with melted butter and set in a warm place until almost doubled in size. Preheat the oven to 375°F.
4 Bake for about 45 minutes, until well-risen and browned. Place on a rack to cool. When cool, dredge with confectioners' sugar.

Makes 4
Preparation time: 30 minutes, plus rising
Cooking time: 45 minutes

APPLE CAKE

2 cups self-rising flour
1 teaspoon salt
½ cup butter, diced
1 lb apples, peeled, cored and chopped
½ cup granulated sugar
2 eggs, beaten
⅛ cup firmly packed brown sugar

1 Preheat the oven to 400°F, and lightly grease an 8-inch cake pan.
2 Sift the flour and salt together into a bowl. Rub in the butter until the mixture resembles bread crumbs. Mix in the apples, granulated sugar and eggs. Pour the batter into the pan, level the top and sprinkle with brown sugar. Bake for 30–40 minutes. Let the cake shrink slightly before turning out. Place on a rack to cool.

Makes 1 x 8-inch cake
Preparation time: 15 minutes
Cooking time: 30–40 minutes

MADELEINES

½ cup butter or margarine
½ cup sugar
2 eggs, lightly beaten
I cup self-rising flour
a pinch of salt

To Decorate:
4 tablespoons apricot or raspberry jam,
whole pieces of fruit removed
I cup shredded coconut
candied cherries
candied angelica, cut into diamond shapes

1 Preheat the oven to 425°F, and grease 2–3 muffin tins (18 cups).
2 Cream the fat and sugar until light and fluffy, then beat in the eggs gradually. Sift the flour and the salt together, fold into the creamed mixture with a metal spoon, and mix thoroughly. Half-fill 18 muffin cups and bake in the center of the oven for 12 minutes, or until firm and golden brown. Transfer to a wire rack to cool.
3 Heat the jam gently to soften it. Spread the coconut on a flat plate. Insert a fork into the base of the cakes to hold them. Spread the jam over the top and sides, then roll the sides in the coconut, pressing it on firmly with a spatula. Sprinkle a little on top, and decorate each cake with a candied cherry and candied angelica.

Makes 18
Preparation time: 20 minutes
Cooking time: 12 minutes

CARROT CAKE

⅔ cup firmly packed light brown sugar
6 tablespoons clear honey
1 ⅛ cups grated carrots
⅔ cup raisins
⅓ cup chopped dates
¾ teaspoon grated nutmeg
½ cup butter
⅔ cup water
I egg, beaten
I cup all-purpose whole-wheat flour
I cup all-purpose white flour, sifted
2 teaspoons baking powder, sifted

Frosting:
⅓ cup butter, softened
6 tablespoons cream cheese
I ½ cups confectioners' sugar, sifted
½ teaspoon vanilla extract

1 Preheat the oven to 350°F, and grease and flour a deep 9-inch cake pan.
2 Mix the sugar, honey, carrots, raisins, dates, nutmeg, butter and water together in a saucepan. Bring to a boil and simmer for 5 minutes. Turn into a mixing bowl and let cool.
3 When cool, stir in the egg (if too warm, the egg will curdle). Mix the flours and baking powder together, sprinkle over the mixture, and combine. Turn into the cake pan, smooth the top with the back of a metal spoon that has been dipped in hot water, and bake for 55 minutes or until firm. Transfer to a wire rack to cool.
4 To make the frosting, beat the butter with the cream cheese until light. Beat in the sugar and vanilla extract. Spread the frosting over the cake and drag the prongs of a fork through it to create a rough-textured finish.

Makes 1 x 9-inch cake
Preparation time: 20 minutes
Cooking time: 65 minutes

RASPBERRY DOUGHNUTS

2 teaspoons active dry yeast
scant ½ cup warm milk
¼ cup superfine sugar
2 cups all-purpose flour, sifted
½ teaspoon salt
1 egg, beaten
1 tablespoon butter, melted
3 tablespoons raspberry jam
½ teaspoon ground cinnamon
oil, for deep frying

1 Blend the yeast with the warm milk, ½ teaspoon of the sugar and ½ cup of the flour. Let stand in a warm place until frothy, about 20–30 minutes. In a separate bowl, mix the salt with the remaining flour. Add the yeast liquid, egg and melted butter, and mix well.

2 Knead the dough on a lightly floured surface, and divide it into 8 equal pieces. Roll each piece into a ball, then press each ball down on the table to make slightly flattened round shapes. Cover with greased plastic wrap and let rise at room temperature until double in size, about 30 minutes.

3 Remove the plastic wrap. Make a hole in the center of each doughnut with the greased handle of a wooden spoon. Fill the hole of each doughnut with 1 teaspoon of jam, and pinch the dough together to seal the hole.

4 Mix the remaining sugar and cinnamon together and set aside.

5 Heat the oil in a deep saucepan or deep frying pan to 370°F, or until a small cube of bread dropped into it browns in 1 minute. Lower the doughnuts carefully into the hot oil and fry for 4 minutes. Remove with a slotted spoon, drain on crumpled paper towels and roll in the sugar and cinnamon mixture.

Makes 8
Preparation time: 15–20 minutes
Cooking time: 4 minutes

MARBLED BROWNIES

1 cup butter, softened
1 teaspoon vanilla extract
¼ teaspoon almond extract
2 cups sugar
4 eggs
2 cups flour
½ teaspoon salt
2 cups chopped almonds, pecans,
walnuts or Brazil nuts
2 oz bittersweet chocolate, chopped

Frosting:
1 ½ cups confectioners' sugar, sifted
1 tablespoon unsweetened cocoa
½ teaspoon vanilla extract
½ teaspoon cinnamon
1 teaspoon butter, softened
1 tablespoon hot water

1 Preheat the oven to 350°F, and grease and line a 9 x 13-inch cake pan.

2 Cream the butter, vanilla and almond extracts, and the sugar until light and fluffy. Add the eggs 1 at a time, beating well after each addition. Sift the flour and salt together and stir into the creamed mixture with the nuts, mixing thoroughly. Divide the mixture in half.

3 Melt the chocolate in a heatproof bowl over a saucepan of simmering water, stirring constantly. Stir the melted chocolate into half the batter.

4 Drop the dark and the light batter by alternate spoonfuls into the cake pan. Cut down and across through the batter several times with a round-bladed knife to give a marbled effect. Bake for 45 minutes, or until a toothpick inserted in the center comes out clean. Transfer to a wire rack to cool.

5 To make the frosting, combine the confectioners' sugar, cocoa, vanilla extract, cinnamon and butter. Stir in the hot water, a little at a time, to give a good spreading consistency. Frost the cake when it is cold, and then cut it into brownies.

Makes 24
Preparation time: 20 minutes
Cooking time: 45 minutes

FUDGE BROWNIES

I cup butter, softened
2 cups sugar
3 eggs
I teaspoon vanilla extract
4 oz bittersweet chocolate, chopped
I cup flour, sifted
½ teaspoon salt
I cup chopped walnuts, almonds or pecan nuts

1 Preheat the oven to 350°F, and grease and line a shallow 9 x 13-inch cake pan.

2 Cream half the butter with the sugar until light and fluffy. Add the eggs 1 at a time, and beat until light. Stir in the vanilla extract. Melt the remaining butter and the chocolate in a heatproof bowl over a saucepan of simmering water, stirring. Let the chocolate mixture cool, then combine with the butter and sugar mixture. Stir in the flour, salt and nuts.

3 Pour the batter into the cake pan, and bake for 45 minutes or until a toothpick inserted in the center comes out clean. Let the cake cool in the pan, then cut into brownies.

Makes 24
Preparation time: 15 minutes
Cooking time: 45 minutes

CHOCOLATE BROWNIES

½ cup butter
⅔ cup firmly packed brown sugar
2 eggs
I cup self-rising flour
4 oz semisweet chocolate, chopped
¼ teaspoon baking powder
¾ cup walnuts or pecan nuts, chopped

I Preheat the oven to 350°F, and grease and line a shallow 8-inch square cake pan.

2 Cream the butter and sugar together until light and fluffy. Beat in the eggs 1 at a time, adding 1 tablespoon of flour with the second egg.

3 Melt the chocolate in a heatproof bowl over a saucepan of simmering water, stirring. Stir it into the butter and egg mixture.

4 Sift together the remaining flour and the baking powder, and fold it into the chocolate mixture with the walnuts.

5 Turn the mixture into the cake pan and bake for 30–35 minutes. Cut into squares while still warm, and let cool in the pan.

Makes 16
Preparation time: 15 minutes
Cooking time: 30–35 minutes

DOUBLE CHOCOLATE CHIP MUFFINS

¾ cup butter or margarine, softened
I cup sugar
3 eggs
I teaspoon vanilla extract
I½ cups all-purpose flour
½ cup unsweetened cocoa
2 teaspoons baking powder
½ teaspoon salt
I cup milk
½ cup semisweet chocolate chips

I Preheat the oven to 375°F, and line 2 or more muffin tins (24 cups) with paper cupcake liners.

2 Cream the butter and sugar together until light and fluffy. Add the eggs 1 at a time, beating well after each addition. Beat in the vanilla extract.

3 Sift the flour, cocoa, baking powder and salt together. Add it alternately with the milk to the butter and sugar mixture, beating well until blended. Stir in the chocolate chips.

4 Spoon the batter into the cupcake liners, filling them about half full, and bake for 15–20 minutes.

Makes 24
Preparation time: 10 minutes
Cooking time: 15–20 minutes

PECAN BROWNIES

2 oz semisweet chocolate, chopped
¼ cup butter or margarine
⅔ cup firmly packed brown sugar
½ cup self-rising flour, sifted
⅔ cup pecan nuts, chopped
2 eggs, beaten

1 Preheat the oven to 350°F, and grease and line a shallow 7-inch square cake pan.

2 Heat the chocolate, butter or margarine, and the sugar in a saucepan until melted, stirring.

3 Place the flour and nuts in a mixing bowl, and beat in the eggs and chocolate mixture until smooth. Pour the mixture into the cake pan, and bake for 30–35 minutes, until the cake is just beginning to shrink from the sides of the pan. Cut into squares while still warm and let cool in the pan.

Makes 9
Preparation time: 10 minutes
Cooking time: 30–35 minutes

BLUEBERRY MUFFINS

½ cup blueberries
5 tablespoons sugar
2 teaspoons grated orange zest
1 cup all-purpose flour
1 teaspoon baking powder
¼ teaspoon salt
1 egg
¼ cup sour cream
¼ cup orange juice

1 Preheat the oven to 400°F, and grease 1–2 muffin tins (12 cups).
2 Mix the blueberries with 2 tablespoons of the sugar and the orange zest, and set aside.
3 Sift the flour, baking powder and salt into a bowl and add the remaining sugar. In another bowl, beat the egg, sour cream and orange juice together, then add to the flour mixture and stir in with a few swift strokes. Quickly fold in the blueberry mixture.
4 Spoon the batter into the muffin tins, filling them two-thirds full, and bake for 18–20 minutes, until risen and golden brown. Let the muffins cool in the tins for 2–3 minutes, then turn out and serve immediately.

Makes 12
Preparation time: 10 minutes
Cooking time: 18–20 minutes

MARMALADE MUFFINS

2 cups all-purpose flour, sifted
1 tablespoon baking powder
⅓ cup sugar
a pinch of salt
1 egg
1 cup of milk
¼ cup softened butter
5 tablespoons orange marmalade

1 Preheat the oven to 400°F, and grease 1–2 deep muffin tins (12 cups).
2 Mix the flour, baking powder, sugar and salt together. In another bowl, beat together the egg and milk, then beat in the butter. Add this to the flour mixture, and stir briefly to mix, leaving lumps in the batter.
3 Put 2 tablespoons of batter into each muffin cup, add 1 teaspoon of marmalade, and add the remaining batter. Bake for about 18 minutes, until risen and golden. Serve warm.

Makes 12
Preparation time: 10 minutes
Cooking time: about 18 minutes

BRANDY MUFFINS

2 cups flour
½ teaspoon salt
2 teaspoons baking powder
½ cup firmly packed light brown sugar
2 extra large eggs, beaten
½ teaspoon grated lemon zest
6 tablespoons melted butter
¾ cup milk
2 tablespoons brandy
1 teaspoon vanilla extract
½ cup coarsely chopped pecans
confectioners' sugar, sifted
ground cinnamon

1 Preheat the oven to 400°F, and grease 2 or more muffin tins (18 cups).

2 Sift the flour, salt, baking powder and brown sugar into a bowl. Add the eggs. In another bowl, mix together the lemon zest, butter, milk, brandy and vanilla extract, and add to the flour mixture. Stir briskly, leaving lumps in the batter. Quickly fold in the nuts.

3 Spoon the batter into the muffin tins, filling them about two-thirds full, and bake for 20–25 minutes, until risen and golden brown. Let cool 2–3 minutes, then turn out and sprinkle with confectioners' sugar mixed with cinnamon. Serve hot or warm.

Makes 18
Preparation time: 10 minutes
Cooking time: 20–25 minutes

ENGLISH MUFFINS

1 tablespoon active dry yeast
½ teaspoon sugar
1 ¼ cups warm milk
1 egg, beaten
2 tablespoons butter, melted
1 lb (4 cups) all-purpose flour
1 teaspoon salt

1 Blend the yeast and sugar with half the milk, and set in a warm place until frothy, about 10 minutes.

2 Mix the egg with the remaining milk and the butter. Sift the flour and salt together into another bowl. Add the yeast and egg mixtures, and mix to a soft dough.

3 Knead the dough on a lightly floured surface for about 5 minutes, until it is smooth and elastic. Place it in an oiled bowl, cover and set in a warm place until doubled in size, about 1 ½ hours.

4 Preheat the oven to 450°F, and grease a baking sheet. Roll out the dough on a lightly floured surface to about ¾ inch thick. Using a 3-inch diameter plain cookie cutter, cut out 8–10 rounds. Place on the baking sheet, and bake for 8 minutes. Turn over with a spatula and bake for another 7–8 minutes. Transfer to a wire rack to cool. Serve split and toasted, with butter.

Makes 8–10
Preparation time: 20 minutes, plus rising
Cooking time: 15-16 minutes

TRUFFLES

4 cups cake crumbs
1 tablespoon unsweetened cocoa
2 tablespoons apricot jam, strained
1 tablespoon rum or brandy extract

To Decorate:
3 oz semisweet chocolate, chopped
chocolate sprinkles
candied cherries, halved
confectioners' sugar

1 Mix all the ingredients together to make a soft dough.
2 Shape one-third of the dough into small balls. Melt the chocolate in a heatproof bowl over a saucepan of simmering water, stirring. Coat the truffle balls in the melted chocolate and then roll them in chocolate sprinkles. Place on a sheet of foil to dry.
3 Roll one-third of the dough to ¼-inch thick, cut into 1-inch rounds and place half a candied cherry on each. Cover with melted chocolate. Place on a sheet of foil to dry.
4 Roll one-third of the dough into a thin log, and then slice into small logs. Dust each with confectioners' sugar and mark with a fork to create a log bark effect.

Makes about 1 lb
Preparation time: 20 minutes

PETITS FOURS

2 egg whites
1 ½ cups ground almonds
⅓ cup superfine sugar
a few drops of almond extract
candied cherries or angelica, chopped

1 Preheat the oven to 300°F, and line 2 baking sheets with parchment paper or rice paper.
2 Whisk the egg whites until stiff peaks form. Use a large metal spoon to fold in the ground almonds, sugar and almond extract.
3 Place the mixture in a pastry bag fitted with a ½-inch star tip, and pipe small stars or swirls onto the baking sheets. Decorate each with a small piece of candied cherry or angelica, and bake for 15–20 minutes, or until just beginning to color. Transfer to a wire rack to cool completely. Store in an airtight container.

Makes 20–24
Preparation time: 10 minutes
Cooking time: 15–20 minutes

PEPPERMINT CREAMS

1 lb (4 cups) confectioners' sugar, sifted
2 small egg whites
5–6 drops peppermint extract

1 Place the confectioners' sugar in a large bowl. In another bowl, whisk the egg whites until they foam but are not thick. Stir them into the sugar, and beat with a wooden spoon until the mixture forms a cohesive mass. Continue to beat until the texture becomes smooth and glossy.
2 Add the peppermint extract drop by drop, tasting after each addition and stopping when the flavor suits you.
3 Sift a little confectioners' sugar onto a flat surface, and roll out the mixture on it to about ½-inch thick. Use small cookie cutters to cut out candies in the shape of bells, stars, Christmas trees and candy canes. Alternatively, roll teaspoonfuls of the mixture into balls.
4 Place the candies on a sheet of foil to dry. Turn them over after a few hours, then leave until the next day. Store in an airtight container.

Makes 24–36
Preparation time: about 30 minutes, plus drying

FROSTED FRUIT AND CHOCOLATE NUTS

Frosted Fruit:
fruits such as grapes, redcurrants or pears
I egg white, very lightly mixed
superfine sugar

Chocolate Nuts:
8 oz semisweet chocolate, chopped
whole almonds, pecan nut halves
or cashew nuts

1 To frost the fruit, use a pastry brush to coat your chosen fruit sparingly with egg white. The sugar will stick only to the coating, so to achieve an attractive effect, coat only the top half of each grape in a bunch or paint the top of the pears and streak the bottom half.

2 Put a colander over a large bowl or plate. Place the prepared fruit in the colander and sprinkle with a liberal amount of sugar. Transfer the fruit to a piece of foil or waxed paper to set.

3 To make the Chocolate Nuts, melt the chocolate in a heatproof bowl over a saucepan of simmering water, stirring. When the chocolate has melted, remove the bowl from the saucepan. Use a fork to stir in the nuts in small batches. When the nuts are coated with chocolate, lift them out with the fork and place them on the shiny side of a sheet of foil to set.

Preparation time: 15 minutes, plus setting

GRAPES IN CHOCOLATE

I large bunch of green seedless grapes
4 oz semisweet chocolate, chopped
½ teaspoon safflower oil

1 Use scissors to cut each grape singly, leaving a short stalk.

2 Melt the chocolate in a heatproof bowl over a saucepan of simmering water, stirring. As the chocolate melts, add the oil, stirring until it is melted and smooth.

3 Holding the grapes by their stalks, dip them 1 at a time into the chocolate so that they are two-thirds covered. Place the grapes on the shiny side of a piece of foil to cool and set.

Makes about 60 grapes
Preparation time: about 25 minutes, plus cooling

MINI BROWN SUGAR MERINGUES

½ cup superfine sugar
⅔ cup firmly packed light brown sugar
4 egg whites
1 ¼ cups whipping cream, whipped
canned or frozen raspberries,
thawed, to serve

1 Preheat the oven to 250°F, and line 2 baking sheets with parchment paper.
2 Sift the sugars together twice. Whisk the egg whites until stiff and standing in peaks. Whisk the sugar into the egg whites a little at a time, making sure the meringue is stiff before each addition.
3 Put the mixture into a pastry bag fitted with a star-shaped tip, and pipe swirls onto the baking sheets. Bake for 1 hour, reverse the baking sheets, and continue baking for 1 hour more, until the meringues are firm and dry, and easily removed from the paper.
4 Let cool completely. Use immediately or store in an airtight tin.
5 Sandwich pairs of meringues together with whipped cream, and serve with a bowl of raspberries.

Makes about 20
Preparation time: 15 minutes
Cooking time: about 2 hours

APRICOT LEATHER

1 ½ cups dried apricots, rinsed
1 drop almond extract
¼ cup sugar
vegetable oil
confectioners' sugar

1 Put the apricots in a saucepan and add enough water to cover them by 1-inch. Cook for about 30 minutes, until very soft. Strain the fruit, discarding the liquid, then purée it in a blender or food processor. Add the almond extract and sugar, return the mixture to the saucepan and cook over a low heat for 5 minutes to dry out and thicken, stirring constantly.

2 Preheat the oven to 200°F. Cover 2 baking sheets with foil and grease them well. Divide the apricot mixture equally between the baking sheets, and spread each part into an 8 x 12-inch rectangle about ¹⁄₁₆-inch thick. Smooth out any darker areas, which indicate greater thickness.

3 Bake for about 2 hours or until dry enough to touch but not very brittle. When cool enough to handle comfortably, dust with confectioners' sugar, turn over onto the counter and peel off the foil. Roll up from the long side and cut into ½-inch slices. Store in an airtight container.

Makes about 24
Preparation time: 15 minutes
Cooking time: about 2 ½ hours

PRALINES

I cup granulated sugar
I cup firmly packed light brown sugar
I cup firmly packed dark brown sugar
a pinch of salt
½ cup milk
¾ cup heavy cream
¼ cup butter
2 teaspoon vanilla extract
2–3 cups coarsely broken pecans
or pecan halves

1 Butter a large piece of foil or parchment paper.
2 Combine the sugars, salt, milk, cream and butter in a heavy, deep saucepan, and heat, stirring to dissolve the sugars. Bring to the boil, and boil to the soft ball stage (238°F on a candy thermometer).
3 Remove from the heat and cool for about 45 seconds, then stir in the vanilla extract and pecans. Beat with a wooden spoon until the mixture loses its shine and becomes creamy.
4 Working quickly, drop by tablespoons onto the foil or paper. The pralines will harden as they cool. Serve within hours of making, as praline does not keep well.

Makes about 32
Preparation time: 10 minutes
Cooking time: 15–20 minutes

COFFEE AND WALNUT CREAM

12 marshmallows
½ cup strong black coffee
1 ¼ cups heavy cream
½ cup walnut pieces, chopped

1 Gently heat the marshmallows and coffee in a saucepan, stirring until dissolved. Let cool.

2 Whip the cream until it stands in soft peaks, then carefully fold it into the coffee mixture. Reserve 2 teaspoons of the walnuts, and fold the rest into the coffee and cream mixture.

3 Spoon the mixture into 4 dishes and sprinkle with the remaining walnuts. Serve chilled.

Serves 4
Preparation time: 10 minutes
Cooking time: 5 minutes

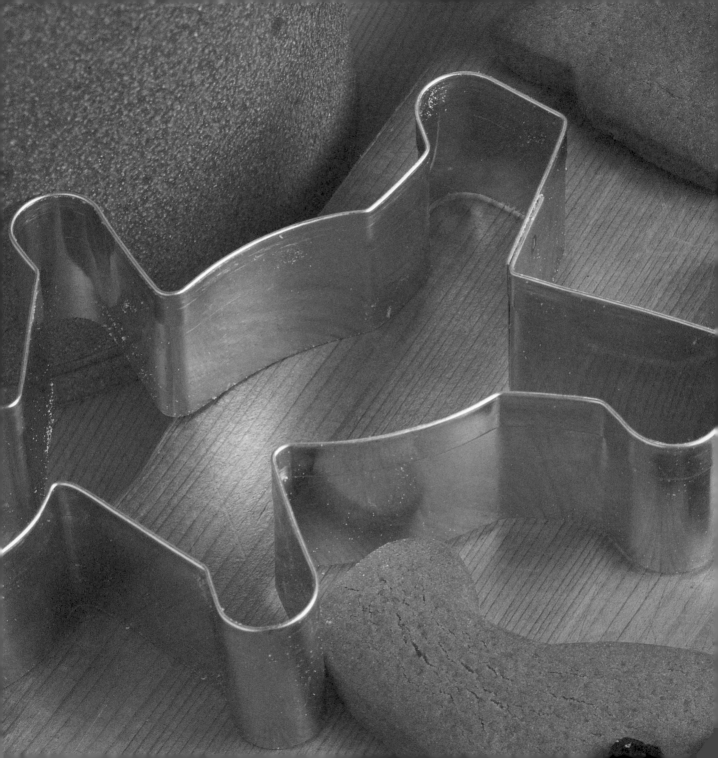